A Mother's Fight
A Faithful God

The Battle was His All Along

By
MJ OKSMAN

To Eric and Jessica, who gave me
both roots and wings.

To my brother, Joe, who always fought for me.

CONTENTS

Prologue vii

Chapter 1   Early Battles 13

Chapter 2   School Battles 19

Chapter 3   Social Battles 27

Chapter 4   Health Battles 31

Chapter 5   Legal Battles 37

Chapter 6   Jail Battles 53

Chapter 7   Personal Battles 77

Chapter 8   Answered Prayers 95

Chapter 9   Hope for the Future 105

PROLOGUE

"I write for the same reason I breathe – because if I didn't I would die." -Isaac Asinov

"Do not be afraid nor dismayed because of this great multitude, for the Battle is not yours, but God's." 2 Chronicles 20:15

"I have called you by your name; you are Mine. When you pass through the waters, I will be with you..." Isaiah 43:1-2

I believe I was born a fighter. When the world would tell me to give in, my faith would make me dig in. Although my life began with having no voice, in time I became a voice and an advocate for many others, especially my son. My battlefield became my blessing field. My wounds have become a part of who I am and only Jesus would make me whole again. I began to realize that only scarred lives can heal and my life's purpose was to share our story with others. This, however, is not just another story of tragedy, but one of triumph. It is not the beginning, but the end that matters. We just have to remember that God is always in control, the plan is always His and the enemy always loses.

As a child I constantly felt like I didn't belong. I was most content being alone in my room, safe from the cruel outside world. Now I realize that God had set me apart, preparing me to become Eric's mom. I learned to trust my inner voice and not others. God was consistently giving me glimpses of the future so I could rise above my present difficulties. Others said I was a dreamer. My father would say I thought too much with my heart and not enough with my head. However, I believe God had given me the ability to transcend my current circumstances by keeping my eyes on heaven while sometimes feeling like I was walking through hell. In the years to come, this would prove to become an invaluable gift.

At an early age, I began to write down my innermost feelings. Journaling became my way of connecting with God when I felt so disconnected with the rest of the world. I found writing every day to be a priceless tool, giving me the insight and courage to get through my most challenging times. Reflecting back on my journals also showed me how God was always working in my life and if He was faithful before I knew He would be faithful again. I no longer felt alone. Journaling gave meaning to my suffering and a way to find a message in my mess. It especially helped me face my son's most difficult trials. When I was too embarrassed to trust this pain with anyone else, I found I could share it with God. Unlike friends, He never judged, just gave me peace and a hope for my future. What I could not get through alone, with His strength I was able to endure. I may have faltered at times, but I never gave up because I knew this is what God was asking of me. When I learned to totally depend on God, He became my partner and was with me always.

Immersing myself in God's word through the years also provided comfort and prepared me for those harder moments. I just had to remember His promise that He who had begun a good work in my son and I would continue it until the end. I was then able to get through difficult times when I began walking by faith, not by sight. I knew God was always there to catch us when we fell because we were His – too precious to drop. Though others often betrayed and abandoned us, He never would. My intent in writing this book with excerpts from my journals is to uplift and encourage others to also fight the good fight, no matter how impossible their circumstances may seem. I believe that is when God can display His greatest power, by making a way where there was no way. However, I have always felt it is not life's difficulties that are the hardest to deal with, but feeling like you are going through them alone. Know that whatever trials come you are not facing them alone.

Be aware though, when God has a plan for your life, the devil will do his best to wipe you out. When

CHAPTER 1

EARLY BATTLES

"Before I formed you in the womb I knew you." Jeremiah 1:5

"I will praise You, for I am fearfully and wonderfully made." Psalm 139:14

"Do not be terrified or afraid of them. The Lord your God who goes before you, He will fight for you." Deuteronomy 1:29-30

*S*o it began. There was a lot of inner and outer turmoil throughout my pregnancy. It was during the late 70s and the economy was much like today. My ex-husband was frequently laid off for long periods of time and my pregnancy only added more stress to an already volatile situation. In addition, I do not think either my ex-husband or I were prepared to be parents, especially to a child that had all the health and emotional issues that Eric was going to have to face. I think Eric felt this in utero and was starting his own fight, because you could literally see him rolling from side to side. Eric was born looking like a prize fighter – screaming and ready for battle. He had difficulty nursing, always putting his tongue on the roof of his mouth. The umbilical cord had been wrapped around his neck, so at first we attributed most of his developmental delays to this. Eric's pinky fingers were bent inward; his facial features reminded me of fetal alcohol syndrome, he had slanted eyes and a flattened nose bridge. I never drank during my pregnancy, yet I wondered if I had done something wrong.

Early on I started asking questions, but never got any answers. Little did I know that I would not get any real answers until 33 years later. The first six months were difficult. Eric never slept, was severely colicky and had projectile vomiting. When I would change

you are close to fulfilling God's purpose that is when you may come under the greatest attack. However, you do not have to fear, because your faithful God will be fighting with you every step of the way.

his diaper, he would cry very loudly. I remember one time when I was changing his diaper, he started screaming and my uncle said, "What are you doing to that kid?" Eric's movements at times seemed spastic. He severely injured his father's eye once when he poked it; another time he shoved a toy plastic bat down his own throat. One thing was certain – Eric never lacked affection. My brother Joe had stopped by once and told my mom that I was kissing him to death. At times he was a very happy baby, making the cutest faces. Looking like Popeye, he would crinkle up his nose and eyes, and all we had to do was say "Eric make your face." Even at 33 years old, he still has a youthful appearance which most have described as elfin-like.

Most of his developmental milestones were delayed, such as not walking until 18 months and not talking until around two years of age. However, he was quick at mimicking motorcycle sounds. He loved big trucks and would squeal with delight when they passed our car. Eric especially enjoyed being in a swing, jolly jumper or anytime he was in motion.

Usually that was the only time he slept. After Eric's sister was born, I began to worry about him harming her, too. The first calamity was when he dropped a night light on her forehead when she was just a month old. Then when she was about 15 months he almost tipped a grocery cart over with her in it. The biggest issue with Eric was his impulsivity, often leaping before he looked. One time my ex-husband, Eric and I were going to see a movie. Before we could stop him, Eric ran down the ramp and fell head first into metal seats. We left and took him to the emergency room. Needless to say we missed the movie. He was constantly falling and sustained many broken bones and head injuries. Over time he broke 8 bones, required stitches 3 times and the emergency room became his second home.

I attempted to get help for Eric early on when his hyperactive behaviors were clearly different from that of most children his age. However, ADHD (Attention Deficit Hyperactivity Disorder) was not commonly diagnosed back then. When he was three years old I remember complaining to mental health professionals that his behavior was not normal and that I was going to lose my mind if I didn't get some answers. They would say nothing was wrong with him.

CHAPTER 2

SCHOOL BATTLES

"For with God nothing will be impossible." Luke 1:37

"Man looks at the outward appearance, but the Lord looks at the heart." 1 Samuel 16:7

"But the very hairs on your head are all numbered. Do not fear therefore; you are of more value than many sparrows." Matthew 10:30-31

*E*ric's first experiences in Catholic School began with a rocky start. He had three different kindergarten teachers. This would have been difficult for any child, but for one with Eric's disabilities, the lack of consistency only compounded his existing problems. Rather than initially recognizing that Eric had a learning disability, his teachers would say that he was not working up to his potential. However, every report card said, "Eric doesn't stay in his seat and has difficulty paying attention." Teachers wanted to blame it on anything and would even make recommendations like changing his diet. One teacher would constantly berate him even withholding treats that all his other classmates would receive. I requested that she find some other way to change his behaviors and to try to see the good in Eric. She replied she really could not see any good in Eric. Of course I was outraged and said that maybe teaching was not the right fit for her. None of these teachers realized what impact these words and experiences would ultimately have in shaping my son's life.

Finally, when Eric started attending public school in the eighth grade, a psychological evaluation was done. He was then diagnosed with a non-verbal learning disability. This translates to him having strong verbal skills, but limited understanding. However, even after the diagnosis, little changed as to how Eric's teachers approached his special needs. He was belittled and bullied by both teachers and peers. He was called stupid, gay and retarded; he was spit on and hit. I lived in constant fear that Eric would be harmed. It was hard for others to accept the ways that Eric was different. However, their lack of compassion and understanding only strengthened my resolve to fight even more for my son. Due to the schools' inaction and refusal to follow Eric's IEP (Individualized Education Plan), I took him to an outside psychologist. This psychologist explained that with this type of learning disability it may appear that Eric had all the nuts and bolts of language, but he was struggling far more than we realized. His performance IQ was superior to only 4% of his peers. Teachers were expecting work that Eric was incapable of doing.

I remember crying after reading this report. I was grateful on one hand to finally get some answers. However, because I had worked with developmentally disabled children myself, I also realized what a struggle life would be for my son. I was to find over time that Eric would also have many health issues as well. On top of everything, Eric had to face adversity at home. My husband had difficulty dealing with the situation altogether and said it would have easier if Eric had physical limitations instead. When he would get poor grades or not stand up to bullies, his father would call him gay and retarded. I told my ex-husband that Eric was a part of him and when he called him names he was calling himself names. A little league football coach even asked me why my husband was so critical of Eric. My ex-husband often blamed Eric for our marital problems. I always believed God had made my son and would work things out. My husband did not share my faith and once stated, "Your God is not going to be able to fix everything." I knew then I would eventually leave because staying would destroy my son and me.

Looking back, I believe if I had not left, Eric and I would not have survived. I am not saying my ex-husband was a bad person, it was just hard for him to accept Eric for who he was. It was easier for me because of my faith and because I had to face so much criticism myself over the years. I knew firsthand what it was like to be abused and to have no one to protect me. Because of that, I feel I overcompensated at times, trying to shelter Eric by making things easier for him so he had at least one person in his corner. Over time school became intolerable for Eric. He said he would commit suicide if he had to go back. When I began to trust God more and more He once again began to guide my steps. I paid attention to the signs and took Eric to a psychiatrist. The psychiatrist diagnosed him with depression. At that time I was fortunate to find out that if that if a school could not meet his special needs, he could be taught at home. The school district did provide a wonderful teacher who finally understood Eric. For the first time someone accepted Eric for who he was and encouraged Eric to accept himself. I am eternally grateful to her.

In time I would find that my biggest challenge was navigating through the healthcare and education systems. There were also very few support networks for parents back then. We tried several medications for the ADHD. With each new medication we were hopeful because initially they helped, but the side effects only compounded his problems. He became more depressed and suicidal and I knew he had to get off them. I would continue to seek guidance from more than 10 health professionals and agencies, including social workers, psychologists, psychiatrists and neurologists, but was never any closer to a workable solution. Eric was tested for Fragile X and Marfan Syndrome, but we could find no genetic component. Although these professionals were able to confirm the school psychologist's diagnosis, they failed to provide us with any meaningful recommendations as how to help Eric succeed despite his limitations. In this way, many professionals had failed Eric and over time this became the hardest thing for me to accept. Being a healthcare professional myself, I also knew that you did not have this many anomalies without a unifying diagnosis. With this mindset and God's Grace I would continue to search for an answer.

Eventually I got divorced and moved when Eric was 18 years old. He still was in high school, so he was able to attend in a different school district that better met his special needs. At 19, with much hard work on his part, he got his high school diploma. However, this move did not come without a cost. We had previously lived in a small country town and I was better able to control who Eric's friends were. When we moved he started choosing friends from more troubled families. This was going to be the beginning of a whole new fight.

CHAPTER 3

SOCIAL BATTLES

"Count it all joy when you fall into various trials." James 1:2

"No weapon formed against you shall prosper." Isaiah 54:17

My grace is sufficient for you, for My strength is made perfect in weakness." 2 Corinthians 12:9

*A*s a young child Eric would go out of his way to assist people by opening doors or carrying packages. He was especially compassionate and helpful to those with disabilities. However, his childlike, trusting nature often led him to surround himself with the wrong people who would take advantage of his kind disposition. For example, as a teenager Eric allowed an acquaintance of his who had just gotten out of jail to stay at my house while my daughter and I were away visiting colleges. This individual then stole from both Eric and me. Eric had difficulty understanding why someone he helped would do something like that. Eric would also say he did not feel comfortable being with anyone his own age so he gravitated toward people that were usually around five years younger than him. I believe Eric chose these types of friends because of his low self -esteem. All of his girlfriends were usually from troubled families and at least one parent was an alcoholic or in prison. These factors contributed to Eric making poor choices that eventually lead to legal problems.

Although Eric loved sports, he did not possess the coordination to really participate in them. He especially loved hockey, but when he tried to join a team he was told he didn't have the skills to play. Eric has not been successful in many areas of his life, but karate is the one sport he has continued to pursue since he was 16 years old. He is only 1 belt away from a black belt. This has not been easy either, since he often is in too much physical pain to practice. He once dislocated his shoulder during a sparring match. However, he continues to stick with karate and I truly believe it has helped him emotionally, mentally and physically

At times Eric would say, "I want to be somebody someday; I want to help people like you do, mom." Of course, with all his limitations finding employment has not been easy, especially now with his additional legal issues. He has had difficulty obtaining and then keeping the most menial of jobs. Jobs that he might have the mental capacity to perform are often too physically demanding. Employers will say he is too slow. Since Eric had a limited awareness of social nuances, he also often becomes the butt of other employees' jokes.

Eric and I have attempted to find a vocation that is a good match for his abilities, but he has received poor guidance from local agencies. Their most recent suggestion was selling magazines. Eric was let go after one week because he could not sell enough. These disappointments have only further decreased his self- esteem. However, I continue to believe God has made my son for a purpose and it will unfold in His time.

It has been difficult for Eric having to see friends and family move on with their lives and experience new opportunities. Yet, I have seen tremendous growth and acceptance in him and it helps me keep going. I have told him how proud I am of the courage and strength he displays every day. Most people will never have to face the challenges he has gone through. I think he is a lot stronger than either of us ever gave him credit for. Ultimately, if he has gotten through these trials, I believe there is nothing in life that will stop him.

CHAPTER 4

HEALTH BATTLES

If God is for us, who can be against us? Romans 8:31

Come to me, all you who labor and are heavy laden and I will give you rest. Matthew 11:28

Trust in the Lord with all your heart and lean not on your own understanding; in all your ways acknowledge Him, and He shall direct your paths. Proverbs 3:5-6

*E*ric soon started developing other health issues in addition to all the broken bones. None of these by themselves would prove to be significant, but a constellation of so many problems again made me question what the root cause could be. At 16, Eric's back went out. Doctors could find nothing wrong, but he was unable to walk for about two weeks. He was also diagnosed then with a mitral valve prolapse. A few weeks later he was diagnosed with costochondritis. Eric also started having gastrointestinal problems at this time. It was Thanksgiving when the symptoms first started and we attributed them to him over eating. Another time his primary doctor thought it was his appendix and had us take him to the Emergency Room. I truly believe this was the start of gallbladder disease that he wouldn't be diagnosed with until he was 25. Eric would frequently become doubled over in pain late at night. I would take him to the Emergency Room, telling them we thought it was his gallbladder. They said, "It can't be; he is not female, fat, fertile or over 40." None of the tests would show anything either. This was another instance when I knew something was wrong, but no one believed us. Over time, with Eric and other family members, I looked to God to direct our path because the healthcare system continually let us down.

After four trips to the ER a Dr. De Jesus (yes, Jesus) finally said, "It's his gallbladder." Eric's gallbladder was removed at age 25. Over time he would also be diagnosed with Gasteroesophageal Reflux Disease. Of course I attributed a lot of this to the all the anxiety he had to face each day. At 28 Eric's shoulder started dislocating. Once it was when he was just getting out of bed. Another time it became dislocated during a karate class. Due to Eric's developmental delays, he would often make poor choices that would put him in harm's way, causing another dislocation. After it dislocated four times, his shoulder was surgically repaired. In time I would realize this was not a fluke, there was definitely something wrong with Eric's joints. Most recently he was diagnosed with arthritis in his hips. Although he is still so young not a day goes by that he is not is some kind of pain. Eric's limited understanding, low pain tolerance and poor coping skills have made these times even more difficult. During one hospital stay, staff didn't understand when he got upset and made some offhanded cruel remarks, making a bad situation worse. However, with God's Grace we got through these times stronger than before and I believe that is because God was preparing us for the biggest battle of all.

January 7, 2009

Please God; I am scared for Eric. Let his shoulder surgery go well; he has had to face so many difficulties. Be with us; I know if I ask, You will.

January 10, 2009

Thank You; last night was a better night. I pray each day that Eric has less pain and more patience and we will feel Your presence with every step. Others don't understand how trying these times have been. That is why I put my confidence in You and not man. I know I am supposed to learn something from all of this. Even in this difficulty I have to choose to bring a little heaven here until I can be with You in Paradise.

April 9, 2009

Please God, Eric is in so much pain. I know You created him and the creation can't be separated from the creator. I know if You can take my son from this place of impossibility we can only give glory to You.

CHAPTER 5

LEGAL BATTLES

"For God has not given us a spirit of fear but of power and of love and of a sound mind." 2 Timothy 1:7

"…rejoice in hope of the glory of God. And not only that, but we also glory in tribulations, knowing that tribulation produces perseverance; and perseverance, character and character, hope." Romans 5:2-4

"We are hard pressed on every side, yet not crushed; perplexed but not in despair; persecuted, but not forsaken; struck down but not destroyed." 2 Corinthians 4:8-9

s I previously mentioned, because of Eric's low self-esteem he tended to gravitate toward younger friends. Due to his immature thinking processes he would often make poor choices. In an effort to fit in, he also was easily persuaded by the crowd. All these factors eventually led him to a decision that would end up in a battle fighting for his life. Eric's legal issues began in January, 2006. He would have to appear in court five times before he was finally sentenced to 10 years of probation on 12/20/06. During this time period Eric had to meet with probation on a weekly basis. Probation was also allowed an unrestricted search of our home at any time. Initially I felt there was no way I was going to be able to handle them showing up wearing guns and going through all our personal stuff. I would have an anxiety attack with every visit. Over time what I found was I just could not handle it in the beginning. Although you never get used to this invasion of your privacy, we began to accept it. It also beat the alternative of jail.

Probation was extremely restrictive; there were many things Eric could no longer do and places he was not allowed to go. In time he would violate one of the rules and we ended up having to return to court. I was constantly praying that the judge and probation office would see Eric the way I saw him. I just wanted someone to give him a second chance. This began some of most heartbreaking, gut wrenching times of my life. In addition, there was always the constant fear looming over our heads that at any time he could still have to go to jail. It was only my journaling that got me through it.

February 14, 2008

Eric violated probation; we have to return to court. The judge is allowing probation to continue. Thank you God for not letting Eric go to jail.

February 15, 2008

I wake up depressed and anxious, worried about Eric's future. Then God says I must trust Him. The devil wants to steal my joy and plants these thoughts in my head. I must not worry about tomorrow because tomorrow will take care itself. I only have today. God knows my heart and He knows I would give up my life for my son. I have to remember I cannot be fearful and still experience joy. Did not God bring me this far? Will He not continue to meet my needs?

February 16, 2008

I am asking You, God – please give meaning to our suffering. Release us from this bondage. Nothing is too hard for You. Let me be able to look back one day and know all this has happened for a reason.

February 24, 2008

How often I forget that just like I don't always give Eric what he wants because it is not good for him, You also do not answer my prayers because it is not in my best interest. I just have to keep my eyes on You during this storm. When Peter walked on the water, he sank when he took his eyes off of Jesus. I must continue keep my eyes on You and Your Kingdom. God has promised me I was created for His glory. I must not remember former things (that is, when I am resentful), because God is doing a new thing in Eric and I.

March 8, 2008

I am reading about the woman at the well and how she suffered. Are you asking me to suffer because those are the ones You always came to? You were the only one who always understood them.

March 10, 2008

I know you gave me Eric for a special reason. We both have something to learn from this because I know You value us both. Please do meaningful work through us with the gifts and talents only we have.

March 13, 2008

Yesterday, I was so tired I just wanted to give up again. I reminded myself that You will meet today's problems with today's strengths and that I should not worry about getting through tomorrow. I just have to do the right thing for Eric and You will provide for us both. Lord, why do I always find such comfort in your words? That is why I believe You left the Bible to us, so Your words could give us encouragement when You physically could not be here.

March 19, 2008

I know my greatest gift would be to give up my son to You just as You did. Since Eric does not understand the way Jesus did, I will gladly sacrifice myself.

March 20, 2008

Eric has to return to court. With so many praying for Eric, I have to believe it is going to okay and just keep my eyes on You. It ain't over 'til it's over. I will praise You even in the storm.

March 21, 2008

The one who loves You is overwhelmed with all I have to do for my job, Eric and my mom. Please give me peace and reassurance that it all will work out and just to take it one day at a time. You reminded me "My grace is sufficient for you; My power is made perfect in your weakness. Therefore, I will boast about my weakness so that Christ's power may rest in me." Again You are saying Eric and I do not have to do this alone and that one day we will be able give glory only to You.

April 1, 2008

Why have I decided to put a limit on God? Are not all things possible with Him? All I ask is to put my son and I where we can do the most good. Please give him a purpose.

April 2, 2008

Lord, please; I know You feel my pain. Every time I am belittled it reminds me of when I was a kid and never loved for who I was. I can handle it, but please make the path smoother for my son. As You care for the sparrow, I know You care for us.

April 19, 2008

My dearest Lord at this moment I am at peace. Is that not what I had prayed for, begged for? You have answered my prayers. I am in a state of grace. No matter what is happening around me, I am okay. Nothing has changed, but everything has changed. Now this is what I pray for my son.

April 22, 2008

Dear Lord, help me not to give up on Eric, although I am so tempted to do so. Just like You never give up on us, eventually the seeds You and I have planted will root and grow.

May 18, 2008

Last night I read without God we have no hope. Life is a relationship with God, the source of all life. We are never beyond Your reach, no matter how isolated our circumstances make us feel.

June 16, 2008

Just like You were not the Messiah others expected, help me to realize what blessings You have for me might not be what I expect.

July 3, 2008

Worry is a lack of gratitude for the way God has provided for me in the past. Did God not provide my children, my career, and my house? Will He not continue to meet my needs? Our enemies can't keep us from what God wants to do through us. I continue to pray for wisdom and peace.

July 4, 2008

Today I awake kind of sad and lost. Is it we do not have what we need here because we do not belong here?

August 14, 2008

Eric returns to court; he will have to go to jail for three weekends. God **where** are You in all of this? I am numb with worry.

February 3, 2009

Be with Eric at probation today. These weekly appointments are difficult now with his shoulder being in a sling, their lack of compassion makes it even more unbearable for him. You remind me what the world has overlooked, my Father has remembered. Life is hard, but God You are great. Life has not been fair, but You are faithful. I will continue to trust You even when trusting You is the hardest thing of all.

February 20, 2009

On this day that my son was born, please bless him. I know You have made him for a purpose. Just like Your Son did not begin His real work until the age of 30, help Eric to begin his real work also. I know You are setting up events to get us where You want us both to be. Help us both to continue to become new creations in Christ. I know You can change everything in an instant; You just have to say the word.

May 13, 2009

God's delays are not God's denials. I had asked that Eric's probation officer would show more compassion with Him. Yesterday I could see she does care about him.

June 26, 2009

Eric had to return to court again for another probation violation. It didn't go as well as I had hoped, but at least he doesn't have to go back to jail. He is miserable with all the limitations this has put on him, but if he violates again he is the one who is going to have to live with it. You are the God of second chances; help him to want to stay out of jail. God please continue to give me the courage to face this heartbreak. I know You want me to tell others my story to show what great things You have done for me.

October 31, 2010

Eric violated his probation yet again. I try to believe

this is all happening for a reason and You will work it out for good.

December 8, 2010

I continue to feel so sad and so hopeless. Eric is so frustrated with all these restrictions. I feel like we have lost all the ground we gained so far. I am so tired of fighting the fight; please God help me to see it through Your eyes. (Then the song "Only You Can Save" started playing in my head.) A part of me wonders whether I would be able spare my son this pain if I didn't love You so much. I know that is what the devil wants me to think – to deny You and then he would leave us alone. God, if it is not in Your will to change our circumstances right now, please change our attitudes.

December 13, 2010

God, Eric is Yours please promote him now, let him find a job maybe then he will not have to go back to jail.

December 16, 2010

Please be with my son as he goes to probation

today. Soften the probation officer's heart God; only You can do that. You have done it before. Help her to see Eric as You see him. I surrender all to You. I do not have to rely on my own power. This is a God thing, not a man thing.

December 20, 2010

I know Eric needs to learn to comfort himself, but if he could have just one success... I am begging God, please let him at least find a job. I know in six months this will all make sense, but right now it is just too much to bear. I just read, "If you want to hear the birds sing, open the window." I do want to feel joy again; please tell me what I need to do to open the window. I will not let Satan win. You will turn this all around. Hope is a good loser, because it knows it will have victory in the end.

December 25, 2010

Happy Birthday, Jesus. You encounter us where we are because You are Emmanuel. You also accept us the way we are, but love us too much to leave us that way. I love You.

December 27, 2010

Sadness seems to come in waves, but I know we need to look below the surface of events to see God's purpose. Failure is not what You have in mind for me. You want the best for us. When I doubt, I am not trusting Your promises. You will continue to lead us on a path that is uniquely meant for us.

January 1, 2011

Even though things seem so dark now, I am reminded Crisis = Danger + Opportunity. Will all the problems we are facing now mean so many more opportunities? What is it God, what are You asking of me this year? Is anything not possible with You? I must not see how big my difficulties are, but how great my God is. I am asking You – spare my son from jail and we will dedicate our lives to You.

January 5, 2011

Someone made a negative comment to Eric about his legal issues. It is so difficult for him to keep paying for the same mistake over and over again. Though others judge us, I know You do not and nothing will ever keep us from Your love. What the world forgets... the Father remembers.

January 6, 2011

Please God be with my son at probation today. Help him find a job. At times this world holds no satisfaction for me; I long to be with You. If I cannot be with You, help me to bring Your Kingdom here; not just for me, but for others as well.

January 10, 2011

Again, I'm feeling life is not fair. My niece is going to Princeton, but I all ask is my son doesn't go to jail. However, I know You want the very best for all of us. Fear and faith cannot coexist. I am scared for my son, but Jesus I trust in You. I just read: "If you are not fighting a battle, chances are you are not fulfilling God's purpose in life and Satan will probably leave you alone."

February 2, 2011

Lord, I see so much courage in my son now. He is displaying so much strength at every turn even when he continues to be knocked down.

February 11, 2011

I haven't written in days because I am too broken by the newest outcome. Eric is going to have to go to jail on weekends again, but this time for six months. Still, the plan is God's and the outcome still His too. I still believe it is in places of greatest difficulty You will show Your greatest power. I am hoping he won't have to go for as long as they are saying. I am praying for a Lazarus moment, when You waited until he was already dead. "We have to celebrate because this brother of yours was dead and is alive again."

February 18, 2011

It has been said common thread with victims is their loss of self-worth and control. However, we know whose we are and who is in control – You – although things appear bleak in the natural in the supernatural all is well. I even told Eric's attorney I am hopeful that the sentence won't be as long and he said, "You are always hopeful." I guess I couldn't ask for a better testament to my faith in You.

February 20, 2011

Happy Birthday, Eric. God's timing is always perfect; even if it seems like something terrible is happening, You will use it for something good. There is a song playing in my head "Be still, because even when it seems like everything is falling apart, He was, He is and He always will be holding me." I'm still praying the judge will find favor with my son and decrease the sentence.

February 25, 2011

I am so far down I can't look up. I am thinking getting through three weekends destroyed me; how will we ever get through 26? I remembered: "today's strength for today's problems". You also reminded me, "Do not be discouraged; God will be with you wherever you go." You will go with us wherever we go. You will go before us this weekend and every weekend. I will give my fears to You and remember I am here to give You the glory.

CHAPTER 6

JAIL BATTLES

Often the test of courage is not to die but to live." Orestas

"I can do all things through Christ who strengthens me." Philippians 4:13

For He shall give His angels charge over you, To keep you in all your ways" Psalms 91:11

We know all things work together for good to those who love God and to those who are called according to His purpose." Romans 8:28

*R*aising Eric proved to be more challenging than I had ever anticipated and these last battles were the most difficult. Eric ended up going to jail two separate times, once in August 2008 for three weekends and the second time in March 2011 for 26 weekends. In one terrible instant our lives had been completely and irrevocably changed. It had been gut wrenching enough to see my son's day to day struggles, but to see him in jail was more than I could bear. It took herculean effort at times not to just run away. In fact I had even contemplated a double suicide if Eric had to go to jail. I was certain that because of his limited understanding he would be at an especially great risk in this environment. There were very few people I could share this with. When I did, as you will see from my journals, their remarks were often caustic and insensitive. As in the book of Job, I began to also protect myself from my so-called comforters. The first weekends were the most diffi-cult because of the unknown. I only had one friend who had experienced jail and she painted a horrible picture. I hibernated on these first weekends because I could not enjoy anything while my son was suf-fering. There was no way I felt we could survive it, yet with God's grace we did.

In sharing the following journal entries I hope it will help things that happen in life seem less random. From them you can see God had been orchestrating events to prepare me to be able to handle what was to come. Knowing that God was still God and was still in the midst of all our trials was what got me through. I would in time believe these troubles were blessings that ended up sparing Eric from something worse. During this ordeal I felt as if a part of me had died. However, because God's glory met my suffering I was still alive. If the words on these pages resonate with you, you will realize that you are not reading this book by coincidence, but it may be an answer to a prayer. God often encouraged me with a scripture verse, another person or a Christian song whenever I needed it most. I found that answers sometimes came in unexpected ways and often it was strangers that offered us the most comfort.

August 3, 2008

Lord, I am so scared. Please don't let Eric go to jail. I know the devil is working overtime to take away my peace. With Your grace I can become transformed to handle this. Help me to remember whose I am and who I am called to be.

August 9, 2008

The brash, flashing lights of the world have to be shut out before I can truly see the purifying light of heaven.

August 13, 2008

The closer it gets to Eric having to return to court for sentencing the more nervous I get. Lord I know when I worry about tomorrow I am being like the Israelite's who tried to collect manna for more than one day. God always gave them what they needed for each day and if they took any-more it rotted. I must not worry about tomorrow; tomorrow will take care of its self. I cannot lean on my own understanding, but trust only in You.

August 14, 2008

Going to court today for Eric's sentencing will be a real test of trust. I believe everything is going to be okay because You are with us. I feel like over the last few days I have experienced a healing that could only come from You. Even though circumstances didn't change, I am changing because You are preparing me for what is to happen next. I am also grateful because normally Eric and I would go to court alone. This time however, Eric's cousin is going with us.

August 15, 2008

My worst fears are realized, yet for once I still trust You God. The judge sentenced Eric to three weekends in jail. I told God He would have to protect my son. Then I read the scripture "For He orders His angels to protect you wherever you go" right on the page of my journal. Today is also the feast of the Assumption the day when Mary goes to heaven. Mary please watch over my son. Also, I read that God never puts you in the wrong place to serve Him. I feel so empty, so scared; please help me. I have to believe though that I did not become as upset at first because like Job, God gave me a glimpse of light at the end of the tunnel. Even though he is going to jail, everything is going to be alright. You will keep Your promise and give me help from on high. Whether I am experiencing blessings or trials, God is working out His purpose in our lives, but Lord, how I long for some blessings. Somehow of late my trials have been many, yet my blessings few. I know I should not feel that way, but I do. I know though that You can change my mind again. God please, You alone can sustain me. I want to take Eric's place, like Jesus took ours.

August 16, 2008

If people would have told me I would be visiting my son in jail I would have said they were crazy. I had to make sure he got through the first night. Lord, this is surreal; being in this environment is so scary. There are so many rules and regulations you need to follow in order to visit. It is the other visitors that are helping me to navigate through. You can't wear any jewelry, cuffs, orange clothes, hoods and the list goes on. I have to maintain eye contact only with

Eric and speak only to him. I am not allowed to touch him. Finally I see him amongst this sea of orange that all the inmates are wearing. The pain I feel is unbearable. Eric looks exhausted. If I feel threatened being in here I can't imagine how he feels. I have to remember when we cry, You cry with us.

August 17, 2008

I was so angry yesterday because at first I was turned away from seeing Eric. I didn't have the right documents with me. I had to drive all the way back home to get them. It was so hard when I did see him. If God protects him through this it may be the turning point for him and me. I get so depressed and discouraged; I definitely do not feel like I am living. One friend said this is temporary, but she has not had to live my life with one problem, betrayal and disappointment after another. I worry it will never end. I know I shouldn't think this way, but I know I can think that way with You. Your mercy is new every day. Just as I always forgive Eric, You will forgive me. Another friend whose brother is a guard says that jail isn't so bad. I said that is because he is on the other side. Still a different friend said that is what Eric gets for violating parole (he is on probation). They have no idea of what they speak and definitely have no compassion. The other visitors at jail said I would find out who my real friends were during this time. Please, God help me to beware of my comforters.

August 18, 2008

I know this is happening for a reason, but I am so tired of the struggle. Others' lives seem to go so smoothly. They don't understand, but I must remember nothing can separate me from Your love unless I allow it to. By today's end I hope I feel Your presence again; I know all I have to do is ask. However, I am so miserable I don't want to, yet I don't want to continue to be in this pain either.

August 19, 2008

Yesterday, I was so depressed and so hopeless, it was as if I couldn't see anything that could bring me joy again. Now that Eric is home safe and one weekend behind us I am hopeful again. I believe that is because people are praying for us. Thank You for the other inmates who invited Eric to attend their Bible Study. They call it God's Table. I can already see how You are using even this for good. I must also remember that You have the final say. Faith is believing what God says, God will do. Eric is Yours and You will take care of him. All is well.

August 20, 2008

Today I was reminded that even in Your day, You did not mingle with the rich and saints, but the poor and the sinners. You always came closest to the ones who needed You the most. That is what I am feeling again today. Did I have to come to a place of such impossibility to show others that it is only by Your grace I can get through it?

August 21, 2008

I just read "Long Walk – Part of the Gift". I believe You are telling me all these difficulties I am facing right now are part of my life too, until I reach the gift of heaven. Thank You for restoring my faith, for helping me forget about my own problems by using me to help others. I feel joy again. I know You still have a purpose for Eric and me. It does not matter what others think, only what You think. I will not seek the false security of the world; You alone are my comforter. Though others reject us, You will not.

August 22, 2008

Please continue to give Eric and me the courage to face this heartache; although this is unfair, to rise above it. Give my son a renewed hope during these difficult circumstances. Help us to surrender to You completely. I just read, "Tranquility is not the path to growth." I can fight this or believe it is strengthening us for something more. I will bend, but I won't break. Things are not always what they appear. Even when Your tomb was empty it was not over. No one can take away the love I have for You. The worst thing that has happened will be the best thing. I must not forget Your promises. I have been moved from desolation to exaltation.

August 25, 2008

It doesn't matter what is happening on the outside as long as I have Your peace on the inside. No matter what things look like, I will be of good cheer because You have overcome the world.

August 26, 2008

I never wanted to fit in or live by the world's standards. I am becoming even stronger to stand up for what I believe in. By drawing closer to You I can become a new creation. Was this all an unexpected snow to change both Eric and I? I am no longer questioning why I am suffering, but what is life asking of me?

August 31, 2008

Thank You, God that this is the last day of Eric's jail weekends. This was the most difficult thing I ever had to do and I know we never would have survived without You. Please let something good come out of this. Please help my son turn his life around. Please don't let us be trapped in our anger. I must continue to trust You to give us what we need, not just what we want.

September 1, 2008

Eric was so upset yesterday when I picked him up. One of the inmates said to him, "How would you like it if I cracked your head open?" Understandably Eric was scared and angry. I am just grateful he didn't retaliate because I can't imagine going through this cycle again. Please God tell me what You are asking of me. Please let the people in the system see my son for who he is and not keep beating him down. Help me to remember all things are possible with You. If You say so, I won't be afraid.

September 2, 2008

Lord I want to help others, but I am so beat down. Please help me with this burden. I know all I have to do is give it over to You. Help me to fast from worry, anger and resentment. Your love is stronger than anything life brings us.

September 3, 2008

Help me to continue to trust You when that is the hardest thing of all. There may be suffering, but You will be in the midst of it. Those of us that sow in tears will reap with cries of joy. Even though I still don't know where You are leading me, this suffering will not be for nothing. The thing the devil tries to destroy me with God will turn it around to promote me.

September 6, 2008

Unlike Jonah, don't let me be afraid to go where You want me to go. It doesn't matter who is against us because with You all things are possible. I just have to rest in You. I also have to learn that if I ask You to spare us and You give us mercy then I must not be upset when You give the same mercy to others whom I feel are less deserving. Thank you Lord for helping me grow so much. I just have to remain in Your will and leave the outcome up to You.

September 10, 2008

I am so grateful for my relationship with You. I just read, "The closer you are to God, the more you will have a heart for others." Please God help my son to also feel close to You. Remind me to continue to look for You in even difficult situations and that every-thing is unfolding as it should according to Your plan.

Everything we go through will be used later to help someone else with a similar problem.

September 20, 2008

Help me keep my eyes on You because it is then and only then that I will have peace. I need to remember happiness depends on circumstance, but joy comes only from You.

October 7, 2008

Keep me from worry. I just have to do my best and You will do the rest. I won't let the devil take a foothold. You will never forsake or abandon me. It is the heartbroken that You care for so much.

October 13, 2008

I've had an epiphany – Joshua told the leaders, "You have seen many miracles; choose now whom you will serve." I, too, have seen many miracles so I must choose to serve You and only You. You are my God alone; there will be no others before You. You alone were there for me when Eric went to jail.

October 14, 2008

Maybe it is not just about just finding peace, but obtaining heaven. Whatever pain we have to go through here on earth, our joy will be greater in heaven.

November 9, 2008

Each person is given something that shows who God is. Please continue to guide Eric and me to our purpose that will reflect who You are.

November 27, 2008

God, when I asked You to be with me when Eric went to jail you reached down and took hold of my hand. You are still continuing to show that not only are You with us, but that You use everything and nothing is wasted. Yesterday, Eric wanted to visit someone he met in jail. While I was waiting for him I spoke with a wonderful minister who, when I told him Eric's story said, "The devil had meant this for evil and God used it for good."

Eric has violated probation again and is sentenced to 26 weekends in jail. The blessing is he will be finished with probation once these weekends are completed. I had been told by everyone that he would never get off probation early. I especially remember a conversation with his court appointed psychologist when I told him that I was still praying God would get him off probation early. His response was "God can't do that." My response was, "You don't know my God; if He can cure cancer, He can do anything." Again, all these trials would be a testament to God's great power. I cannot and I will not limit God. You never want to put a period where God has put a comma. It is not over until it is over.

March 7, 2011

Eric completed his first weekend and this is harder than I ever could have imagined. How will we ever get through 25 more weeks? God reminded me that I was not alone and He who had been with me during my darkest times was still by my side now. I also saw that Eric's girlfriend had put together a booklet of inspirational quotations for each weekend. I cried tears of joy. She knows it was quotations that have gotten us this far. It reminded me others are watching, so I must continue to reflect You, showing grace under pressure.

March 8, 2011

Eric is so down; my biggest fear is he won't go in this weekend. Then I read, "Trials are gifts from God reminding us to rely on Him alone." I just have lean on You. You are our Father and want what is best for us. Even though my heart is torn, I will praise You in this storm.

March 12, 2011

It's hard to sleep when Eric is away. I wake up worrying, "Is he safe?" At times other people, like Job's "friends", have made me feel that bad things are happening because I am bad. You say that is not the reason. They happen so God's works might be revealed. God please continue to give meaning to my suffering. I know if I ask You will answer. Continue to make Your strength perfect in our weakness.

March 19, 2011

Lord I just realized I am no longer worried, just

sad. I just want to feel some joy again. I still need to believe the best is yet to come. I have read, "The greater the battle, the bigger the blessing." For right now, thank You for protecting my son. You will restore everything to those who have been faithful to You.

March 22, 2011

The one You love is hurting. I know the important thing is to spend eternity with You, but I am so sad and beat down. I love You, but in this moment I feel so alone. I am sure Satan is attacking me and so I just have to immerse myself in Your word even more. Like Solomon, I am asking for wisdom. Don't let me try so hard to hear the shout that I miss the whisper. I believe if You can help me endure this difficulty of Eric's jail sentence, You can help me endure anything. You are telling me to stop trying to work things out before their time. I do not know where You are taking me but I cannot stay where I am.

April 1, 2011

Why do people always say the most insensitive things? I am so depressed and burned out, but they just add insult to injury. I know I can't expect comfort from others; I can only look to You. You remind me that no matter how difficult or impossible my situation is, You will come to me with Your answers and Your comfort. Holy Spirit please continue guiding me to only allow people I can trust into my life, especially while I am in this fragile state.

April 14, 2011

Something has changed; is it because Eric is been more accepting of this cross? How great You are; the person You have set free is free indeed.

April 16, 2011

You reminded me You are my hiding place. Please continue to keep my son hidden in You this weekend.

April 21, 2011

Just when I thought things couldn't get any worse, my mom is in the hospital with pneumonia. I am grateful You made me realize something was really wrong with her. Sometimes I start to wonder how I am ever going to fulfill my purpose when I am always being sidetracked. However, is it not Your purpose for me to serve others? You reminded me the only way I will have peace is to experience it where I am and not wait for everything to perfect, because it never will be. I have to choose it every day and no one can steal my joy unless I allow it.

April 25, 2011

Maybe things had to get worse before they got better. Like Corrie Ten Boom's story about the concentration camps where they had fleas. It was the fleas that kept their captors away from them. Maybe that is what You have done with Eric and you are using these difficulties to protect him from something worse.

May 7, 2011

God on this Mother's Day I only ask that You protect my son.

June 25, 2011

If it is part of your plan that Eric has to continue to go to jail on the weekends, then Your will be done. However, if it's not then let all the right doors open now. I will continue to believe that You have good planned for our future no matter how difficult the present might be. No weapon formed against me will prosper.

July 3, 2011

I have learned that I can handle these weekends only if I remain in Your presence. My security rests in You alone.

July 31, 2011

Sometimes I am still afraid of life's storms. Continue to be with my son and me. I read, "I have called you by name; when you pass through the waters I will be with you and they will not sweep over you." You have saved us before and I know You will save us again. I trust not only that You can, but that You **will** turn our lives around. I will fear nothing and hope everything with Your Grace.

August 15, 2011

I know You will continue to guide me and encourage me by giving me a vision of my future.

Thank You for keeping my son safe during one more weekend. There are only two weekends left; I will rely on Your strength and not mine. You will see us through it. Your power is in me; I just need to remember to use it.

August 23, 2011

I sometimes feel as if I am not enough. I have to remember that You are enough to face any problem, enough to help Eric find his way, enough to take care of my mom. You are my partner and always with me, so I am guaranteed success. With You, Eric and I will climb from the lowest pits (these jail weekends) to the highest heights. It only takes a minute for You to change everything. You have made Eric and will complete the good work You have started in him.

September 4, 2011

Eric has completed his jail weekends. You alone got us through, so much so that Eric had Philippians 4:13 ("I can do all things through Christ who strengthens me") tattooed on his side. One weekend when he was in jail he found that scripture written on the wall above his bed and knew he could not have gotten through this without God. Life has not been fair, but You have always been faithful. Although I often wished Eric and I never had to experience this heartbreak out of it came a new strength and closeness to You and each other.

CHAPTER 7

PERSONAL BATTLES

"Two roads diverged in a wood; I took the one less traveled by and that has made all the difference." -Robert Frost

"But He knows the way that I take; When He has tested me, I shall come forth as gold." Job 23:10

"A man's heart plans his way, but the Lord directs his steps." Proverbs 16:9

*T*his was not what I signed up for. At first I felt like Saul wanting to tell God to choose someone else because I was not up for this job. Since the day Eric was born my life was no longer my own. In addition to dealing with all of Eric's legal problems, I was also constantly assisting him with many other issues. Working with all the agencies and filling out paperwork at times was overwhelming. It always took at least several tries to get Eric the services he needed. I wanted to give up when we did not get the results we had hoped for. I could handle anything except when Eric would lose his temper. I understood his frustration and all the physical pain he was in, but at times I felt this stress was more than I could bear. I was a single mom juggling a demanding job in addition to being my mother's primary caretaker. However, it was Eric's tirades that were the most difficult to accept. It was then I would feel like I was going to have a nervous breakdown. That's when a friend said I wasn't having a breakdown, but a breakthrough. She said I had to take a step up and, like an eagle, soar above my current circumstances.

Often I would pray that God would just give him peace to accept his present situation better. God always answered my prayers and usually by the next day Eric's attitude had improved. Most recently services that we had been fighting for had gotten denied again for the third time. Normally I would have been depressed for days, wanting to give up altogether. God even had His hand on this. I was watching Joyce Meyer when I received the news. She reminded me of John 16:33 "In the world you will have tribulation, but be of good cheer; I have overcome the world." I just had to draw closer to God and He would draw closer to me. Immersing myself in God's word had strengthened my relationship with Him and I knew no matter what things looked like, He would have the final say. I knew that before the trouble had even started God had promised me a victory. That morning I had also contemplated not writing this book. Now I knew I definitely had to because I had to encourage others not to give up like I had wanted to so many times in the past. Although the devil had meant all these difficulties for something bad, God would use them to help me encourage others.

At times I would ask, "God how could You let this happen? Why don't you do something about this?" God replied, "I certainly did do something about it; I made you." Although I may have started out like Saul, I became like David; knowing my God had put seeds of greatness within me uniquely preparing me for this moment. When Eric was about 12 years old I reached out to a teacher friend who told me never to forget how lucky Eric was to have me in his corner. She reminded me that I was his advocate and to never stop fighting for him because that is what we mothers instinctively do. Little did I know how prophetic her words were. Those words were a comfort then and continue to provide me comfort today.

The experience of raising Eric has taught me that you can find your greatest purpose through your darkest times. I was able to find power in my pain. I learned to trust myself and God when I felt no one else was there for us. God was faithful, keeping every promise and meeting every need. When things were at their worst it seems friends and family not only abandoned me, but usually added insult to injury.

However, when I was down to nothing, God was up to something. I learned not to look upon a closed door so long that I missed the ones that were opening. I only needed to rely on Him and remind myself that He would not have brought me this far to leave me now. I no longer relied on my own understanding, but Gods. My greatest adversity built my greatest strengths. I did not need anyone else's validation, only God's. I began walking by faith, not by sight. I was then able to continue fighting the good fight and run the race with endurance that was put before me.

…Although I did not know what my future held, I did know in whose hands it was held and there are no better hands.

I remember when I was starting a class for pastoral ministry I asked a nun at my church, "What if I don't have the right words to say?" She said that all any of us want is to give meaning to our suffering. I have found that so many people are spiritually bankrupt and anxious over so many things. I often felt I could at least encourage them to let go and let God help them find meaning in their suffering. If I was able to touch a few lives just in my everyday interactions, how many more could I touch if I wrote a book? Everything Eric and I have gone through had a purpose and I had to tell our story. Although others always had wanted me to be something I was not, at an early age I realized I had gifts that were mine alone. I believe that I was born for such a time as this and everything I have gone through has shaped me into the person I am today. I had never lived by others' definitions of success and I did not want to start now. I was always dreaming of how things were going to be; not satisfied with how they were. Deep down inside I know I feel the most alive fighting for something I am passionate about. It became my desire to be used by God for His greatest good. I learned that we cannot always fix things for others, but we can lead them to the One who can.

I believe that although I will no longer be working in my chosen profession, I am not empty yet and this is now what God is calling me to do: be a voice for other kids who do not have someone to advocate for them like Eric had me. It is also my desire to raise awareness about chromosomal abnormalities and genetic testing. I hope that our story will encourage other parents to get answers when they believe something is wrong with their children, so they will not have to go through what we have gone through. I hope it will inspire all of us to heal children early so we will not have to spend years repairing the damage. We either pay now or we pay later, but whether it is sooner or later all of society pays. There also needs to be light shed on a legal system that lumps all felons together even when they have disabilities. It should not be "one size fits all". The probation system says their goal is to make them productive members of society, but the current system never lets them forget their offense. Then it becomes a self-fulfilling prophesy, tell them they are not worthy and that is what they become. I especially feel it is imperative to disfavor sentences where hopelessness is a part of the framework, because without hope there is no chance for change.

Through my journaling I began to realize that when facing some of life's biggest challenges, I only had to look to God and myself. I am not able to change the past, but I can change my attitude to improve my future. This journey has given me the insight to be able to accept all these trials, not allowing them to change me, but to ultimately reveal my true character.

September 25, 2005

Eric keeps going off on tirades and I am starting to feel far away from God again. I feel like everything is out of my control. I can't control anything anymore; not Eric, not my feelings, not my world. Dear God, please help me to get my focus back on You and only You. Help me to remember in Your divine plan everything is already in order and it doesn't depend on me. You are not a God of chaos, but peace. Help me to let go of this turmoil in my mind knowing Your grace will sustain me. Replace my anxiety with trust, surrendering to You. Let nothing separate me from You.

May 18, 2007

No matter how much grief Eric causes me, I still love him and want his happiness. Is it not the same with God my Father? He wants me to be happy in this world, but more importantly to be truly happy with Him in the next. God I can lose everything, but please do not let me lose You.

May 30, 2007

Everything I have gone through was what I needed to reach wholeness, to reach heaven. I think I am finally ready to accept that.

June 1, 2007

I believe God is telling me to slow down, to remember what is really important to me. To live as if this might be my last day, not anxious but joyful, continuing to touch as many lives as I can. My hope is that one day sharing my story will encourage others to tell theirs. God you have always given me what I needed when I needed it. I am truly joyful in this moment because I feel I have grown into myself, becoming who I was supposed to be all along.

June 8, 2007

Yesterday was tough; I asked You to take me or be with me. You choose to be with me as You always are. Help me to continue to look for you in the midst of all this pain. I know you are so close to me that when others sense the storm and worry, I will hear Your voice and smile. Tomorrow will be better than today.

June 11, 2007

Blessed are the poor in spirit, for theirs is the kingdom of heaven. It is the poor in Spirit that recognize their complete dependence on God. Is this not where I am? Maybe that is what this was all about – feeling weakness to experience Your strength and reach out to You even more. I must always remember Your promise that You will never leave or forsake us. You will be with us always.

January 10, 2008

During my difficult times I feel like God is testing my faith. However, it really is a test of God's faithfulness, because He always comes through. I've also realized God will sometimes shipwreck our plans in order to get us to where we need to go. I have to remember God's goal is not our comfort, but producing the character of Christ in us so others will be drawn to Him. Help me continue to listen for Your voice in the whispers and the shouts.

January 26, 2008

You are not asking me to be successful, only to be faithful. If I set out in the world to help myself eventually I will help everyone else. I believe God long ago drew a circle around the spot where Eric and I are standing right now. I know I am where I am supposed to be. I just have to continue to look to You for answers; trusting the past to Your mercy and the future to Your providence.

February 14, 2008

Maybe it is good that life has not been so comfortable here because it will not be so hard to leave it. This is not our home and that is why we always have a constant longing. The devil loves to steal our joy and plants worries in my mind. I must not worry about tomorrow; tomorrow will take care of itself. I only have today.

November 30, 2008

I wake up discouraged and then I read about the apostles being asked to leave everything to follow Jesus. I wish I could have had that opportunity, but isn't that what You are asking me every day when I am taking care of my mom and Eric.

December 5, 2008

When the apostles were fishing on the wrong side

of the boat (without Jesus) they couldn't catch any fish. This reminded me when I work outside of God's will, I will not fulfill my purpose. Help me to remain in Your will and remember I don't have to do this alone.

December 27, 2008

I just read that faith is like film: developed in the dark. I know it is all the dark times that have strengthened my faith. Hasn't it been in my worst moments that God gave me my best insights? I can't change my past, but I can change my future with God's grace.

January 4, 2009

I keep thinking if Eric would just change, my problems would all go away… or are You asking me to change and not let it affect me so much? Nothing is too hard for You and You will answer all my prayers in Your time. Though life is not always fair, You are always faithful.

January 21, 2009

I can either let God or be God. When we can't, God can. I will not look at what I lost, but what I have gained. Thank You for giving me a peace that defies logic. If I continue to do Your will, the rest will follow.

March 6, 2009

I worry about getting my fair share. I pray my desire for what God has kept from me will not keep me from enjoying what He **has** given me. I have to remember You call the man, decide the plan and know the span of time needed to bring it to completion. You have authority over everything. You know what I need before I ask and I am never beyond Your reach.

March 15, 2009

Although so many have rejected my son, I have to remember they also rejected You and me. I know You still have a special purpose for him. Please help my son find a job.

March 17, 2009

Lord since You are directing my steps, I do not need to understand everything that happens along the way. I will pray continually with expectant faith even if I do not see my prayers answered right away. My relationship with You is all that matters. You are the only one who is true and constant.

March 25, 2009

Will life always be a struggle? You have said, "In this world You will have problems, but do not fear – I have overcome the world." When I live in the past I have regrets, in the future I have fear. Only when I live the present can I experience Your joy. You do not desire me to be successful, only faithful to Your will. You have always only asked that I bloom where I am planted, doing what I can, where I am with what I have. Then and only then will I have the peace that surpasses all understanding.

April 2, 2009

You tell me not to be afraid or discouraged. Fear is of the devil. He loves to steal my joy. I will feed my faith so my fear will starve to death. If the Lord bids me to fly, I will trust in Him for the wings.

May 16, 2009

God I don't want any more "To Do" lists; I

just want a life. I am feeling overwhelmed again. I know coal is formed by pressure into a diamond, but shouldn't I be one by now? Maybe I need to stop carrying it by myself. I just have to learn to rest in Your Presence, to trust in You when trouble comes. Although I am not who I want to be; I know You are not done with me yet. You will do what I can't. Take my ashes and give me beauty.

June 1, 2009

I feel like I have had my Egypt, my desert, so the only thing left is the Promised Land. I must not give up before I reach it. You will deliver me, but I need to get over all the anger and resentment I still have at times. I can change by living out of my imagination instead of my memory. Help me again to walk by faith and not by sight.

June 26, 2011

I just read that when a player starts to score, the opposing team sends out their best players to block him. I believe that as I get closer to my goals, Satan steps up his attack.

July 18, 2011

Whatever is at the center of your life will be your security, guidance, wisdom and power. Since I have made You the center of my life, I have peace. Being close to You will help me shine brightly in this dark world. I truly feel wrapped in Your love.

October 24, 2011

I've had another epiphany moment; since it is in our weaknesses that we feel closest to You, I shouldn't feel sad that I have had a more difficult life. I should be grateful because I have had a closer walk with You. We have no guarantee that life will not hurt, but I continue to believe that You are mending me in all my broken places until I become the whole person I was always born to be. It is only I that will keep myself crippled and it is only Eric who will keep himself in jail by living in the past.

October 31, 2011

It's gotten to the point that being there for Eric is pure joy because you have changed me. Thank you for the love that has grown for my son, because I need to be here for him.

December 20, 2011

Eric had a meltdown. This time I gave it right to You and You gave me peace. You reminded me I need Your love most when I deserve it least and so does my son. I know it is frustrating for him – his physical pain, not feeling like he has a purpose and seeing others having normal lives. We can't be jealous of what others have, because then we will miss what you have in store just for us. Please give him peace, too and help us not to focus on our problems, but Your power. You are a faithful God.

February 12, 2012

As I look over my journals I realize I could not appreciate the simple, peaceful life I have now were it not for all the pain I had experienced in the past. Although I found myself on a road I did not plan, God stayed beside me with every step I took. God has taught me that when I have been down to nothing but God, God was all I ever needed.

CHAPTER 8

ANSWERED PRAYERS

(God's got this.)

"It is never too late, to be what you might have been." George Eliot

"When the heart weeps for what is lost, the spirit laughs for what it has found."
-Sufi Aphorism

"Do not remember the former things, nor consider things of old. Behold, I will do a new thing! Now it shall spring forth; Shall you not know it? I will even make a road in the wilderness and rivers in the desert." -Isaiah 43:18-19

*G*od was at work in our lives, arranging circumstances to provide an answer. One night I was watching a television program about a chromosomal abnormality called Williams Syndrome. When they described some of the characteristics these individuals had, I realized Eric had most of them. I made an appointment with a geneticist. Although the doctor did not believe Eric had Williams Syndrome, he did feel a chromosomal test was warranted because of all of Eric's developmental and medical issues. This doctor was especially kind and comforting. He said that Eric was special and that is the reason why society may not have been so accepting of him. The test showed that Eric did have a chromosomal abnormality with duplication on one his chromosomes. Individuals with this specific duplication can exhibit developmental delays, anxiety, Autism, ADHD, slanted eyes, a flat nasal bridge and hypermobility of joints. Finally, after all this time we got a diagnosis and now maybe Eric could obtain the services he needed.

Through the years I had longed for answers and someone who could understand what we were going through. Of course we didn't have the technology or support systems that we have today, otherwise I am sure we would have gotten Eric the help he needed much earlier. In fact, the particular micro array test that identified Eric's specific abnormality was not available until 2005. However, I wanted to believe that this all happened for a reason and God's timing again was perfect. I started to surf the web for Eric's particular chromosome duplication (16p13.11) and found it was not uncommon. There was even a Facebook page about a child with a deletion on the same chromosome. There appears to be a large community out there and I am sure we will learn from each other. It is also my prayer that our experiences might help guide others in making future decisions for their children. People who are hurting need to hear from someone who has gone through it. Who can better empathize than us?

The doctor now requested that Eric's dad and I both have the same chromosomal test. The results reflected that I did have the same chromosomal abnormality as Eric but my ex-husband did not. This means Eric had inherited this chromosomal abnormality from me. I believe although I did not have some of the same issues Eric was struggling with, it is what has helped me to understand him better. When we got the results the geneticist said, "God knows which children to put in which families." Of course, as you will see from my journals, I never would have continued to pursue getting answers were it not for God encouraging me every step of way through His scriptures and His people.

June 12, 2011

God, are You trying to show me what is really wrong with Eric? I have always wondered why he has so many anomalies. Last night I saw a show about Williams Syndrome and Eric has a lot of the characteristics. I believe You are guiding me. I am not asking You to take his problems away, only to help us find an answer if there is one. I know You are telling me it will be okay. I will make an appointment with a geneticist.

June 24, 2011

I am praying that with a definitive diagnosis Eric could get out of jail weekends sooner. Even though so many others say it will never happen, they do not understand Your power. They often judge my faith as being radical, but is doesn't matter. I know You were faithful before and will be faithful again. Help us to continue to look beyond our circumstances, remembering nothing is hidden from You and if You want me to have an answer; You will help me to find it. You are the engineer in our lives, designing the best path for us and only us. Nothing and no one can preempt Your Plan. In due season, You will bring it to fruition.

September 23, 2011

Today we are going to the geneticist. I know you have made my son. Please God if there is something wrong; help us to find the answer that I have searched for his whole life. I do believe though, if things had been easy for us, I would not have always looked to You. Our problems forced us to depend on You instead of ourselves. Even though it will be at least a month before we get an answer, I remain hopeful that some of Your richest blessings are around the corner.

October 27, 2011

Prayers asked, prayers answered. The geneticist called and Eric does have a chromosomal abnormality. Finally, it all makes sense after all these years. Now we need to find out if it is familial or not. Thank You, God for directing me every step of the way and reminding me that earth has no sorrow heaven cannot heal. I believe this answer will give me the courage to continue to fight for Eric. So many times others said that I was spoiling him, but I knew as only a mother does that there were some things he just could not understand.

November 10, 2011

Thank you, Lord for the renewed love that has grown in my heart for my son. I know the devil would love to attack my peace, but I just told him to go away. Right now I need to be here for Eric. I just need to draw on Your strength and Your promises. I also believe that because my son and I have been persecuted so unjustly at times, great will be our reward in heaven.

November 12, 2011

I just read about the importance of the word "anyway". Eric has so many obstacles to overcome but I know he will fulfill Your purpose in his life anyway. You are still on the throne and have an appointed blessing for an appointed time for him and me. It's about not letting our problems get in the way of our blessings. You are recreating us both into who we are supposed to be.

December 4, 2011

God, I know you formed Eric. I know all those years he was misunderstood were just setbacks, but You are setting him up for something great. I believe that is why he was not harmed in jail. Thank You for helping me believe in him when no one else did.

December 10, 2011

God continue to tell me what you are asking of me. Show me where Eric and I fit in and help me to see Your hand in all of it.

December 15, 2011

I am disappointed with the help I am supposed to be getting for Eric, but will remember You have the final say. I know there is often a battle going on between good and evil that I cannot see, so I must not lose hope. Though others do not always value us, You do

December 29, 2011

Do I wish Eric did not have all these problems? Yes, but if we didn't have the test, we would not have the testimony. You have led us on a path that was uniquely designed for us. It is the struggles that shape us into who we are supposed to be. Although things may seem hopeless at times, failure is not what you have in mind for us.

January 6, 2012

The geneticist called and told me that I have the same chromosomal abnormality Eric has. He said, "We have to be very wise when we choose our parents and we definitely know you are Eric's Mom." You reminded me that because he is my son I will care for him and because I am your daughter, will You not also care for me? I have nothing to fear.

CHAPTER 9

HOPE FOR THE FUTURE

"For I know the thoughts that I think toward you," says the Lord, thoughts of peace and not of evil, plans to give you a future and a hope." Jeremiah 29:11

"Being confident of this very thing, that He that has begun a good work in you will complete it until the day of Jesus Christ." Philippians 1:6

"Treat a man as he is and that is the way he remains. Treat a man as he ought to be and that is what he becomes."
-Goethe

I have always loved the water, especially watching waves crash against the shore when a storm comes up. Eventually though, God does calm every storm. It reminds me of life's challenges. I can let them overcome me, or hold onto Him and ride the wave. Once I stopped fighting, I was able to channel His power. I have learned that with each difficulty that has come crashing around me, with God's grace I was able to accept it and move on. This journey has shown that trials are not enemies of faith, but opportunities to prove God's faithfulness. Every disappointment brought an appointment to grow closer to God. With every challenge has come a blessing; God had a plan before we had the problem. God doesn't give us tasks equal to what we can do, but equal to what He can do. I believe that everything we had gone through was not God destroying us, but refining us to inspire others. We became the change we desired to see in the world.

Although I was Eric's teacher, he became mine. It may have been hard to ever fight for myself, but I would always fight for Eric. Even when everyone else believed the situation was hopeless, I would fight anyway because I knew that was when God would show His greatest power and we would be able to give glory only to Him. The reward could not be measured, but I believe I began to understand what unconditional love was and how God loves us. Over time Eric and I have helped each other to heal. I once read that being a parent of a disabled child is like being touched by the Divine. I experienced such joy when all Eric's difficulties were finally given a name and that God had chosen me to be his mom. It gave me the courage to continue to fight. Although Eric and I had to start to have different kinds of dreams, I knew that what God had in store for us would be so much better than we ever could have hoped for ourselves. We just had to trust Him.

When I learned to walk in the spirit relying only on God, I became free of all worry for myself and my son, realizing I couldn't reach out for the future if I kept hanging on to the past. Truly I became a new creation, not conformed to this world, but transformed by a renewing of my mind. I no longer prayed for a change in circumstance, but a change in attitude. Then God gave me strength and wisdom that I did not know I had, to no longer be afraid of the storms, because the winds would blow us to where we were supposed to be. I began to understand that my physical circumstances did not have to change in order to feel God's peace. I knew if I continued to remain in His presence, listen to His promptings and remember His promises, all would be well. His power would add Super to my Natural and Extra to my Ordinary to fulfill His purpose for my life and grant me the desires of my heart because He had placed them there. The ending of our story was going to be so much better than the beginning.

Others are often amazed at how I always remained hopeful during such trials. Even a publisher I talked to said, "I am surprised you continue to have so much faith." This always baffled me, because isn't that what faith is? The assurance of things hoped for, the conviction of things not yet seen. Joyce Myer has said faith is being able to live with unanswered questions. For me, God became either everything or nothing. I was not always this way. Initially, I believed I was in charge, only willing to give Him certain parts of my life. It was when I gave God total control that I found peace and became free from worry. Most importantly, over time I started to feel joy again and excitement about our future, even with all the trials we had experienced. What I had deemed as an unthinkable situation I was able to get through with God's grace. Although everything else had fallen apart, God was the one constant. I especially found it remarkable when Eric and I even began to feel love for his probation officer. We realized her intentions were good and she was only doing her job. During this ordeal I felt as if a part of me had died. However, because God's power met my pain I was still alive. I know that it was God and only God who transformed me.

My desire is our journey will show you what God can do if you just ask Him. No matter what trials you are going through, you do not have to go through them alone. It is my prayer that our story will not impart desperation, but inspiration. My vision is to help others gain a better understanding and empathy for those with disabilities. I hope we learn to celebrate others' differences instead of finding fault with them, realizing we are all connected and when one suffers, we all suffer. We don't need to see the end of our stories to see God's guiding hand. We just need to know that those who wait upon the Lord will be blessed. Sometimes blessings in life come early, sometimes they come late, but they always come. Everything will be alright in the end, so if things are not alright now, it is not the end. I have always believed that life is like a football game at halftime – no one is sure who is going to win. I do not know the final outcome of my son's life or my own. What I do know is that my faithful God will be fighting with us every step of the way.

CPSIA information can be obtained at www.ICGtesting.com
Printed in the USA
BVOW041726060313

314878BV00001B/1/P